PLACES IN ART

Clare Gogerty

Artwork: Tony Morris

CHERRYTREE BOOKS

80 001 887 519

A Cherrytree book

Designed and reproduced by Touchstone Publishing Ltd

Copyright this edition © Evans Brothers Ltd 2003
Published by Cherrytree Press Ltd
327 High Street
Slough Berks SL1 1TX

First published in 1994
First paperback edition published 2003

Designer: David Armitage
Cover designer: Simon Borrough

Cover picture: *The Artist's Garden at Giverny*, Claud Monet

British Library Cataloguing in Publication Data
Gogerty, Clare
     Places in Art. – (In Art Series)
     I. Title II. Series
     707

     ISBN 1 84234 177 4

Printed in China through Colorcraft Ltd., Hong Kong

All rights reserved. No part of this publication may be reproduced, stored in a retrieval system, or transmitted, in any form or by any means without the prior permission in writing of the copyright holder, nor be otherwise circulated in any form of binding or cover other than that which it is published and without similar condition including this condition being imposed on the subsequent purchaser.

Northamptonshire Libraries & Information Service	
Peters	17-Apr-03
704.94	£5.99

Contents

In every chapter of this book you will find a number of coloured panels. Each one has a symbol at the top to tell you what type of panel it is.

Activity panel Ideas for projects that will give you an insight into the techniques of the artists in this book. Try your hand at painting, sculpting and crafts.

Information panel Detailed explanations of particular aspects of the text, or in-depth information on an artist or work of art.

Look and See panel Suggestions for some close observation, using this book, the library, art galleries, and the art and architecture in your area.

What is landscape?

Imagine you are in a house in the middle of the country. You look out of a window and you see trees, fields, hills, perhaps a cow or a flock of sheep. Out of another window you see an old bridge, a stream, more fields and a cowshed. These views of the countryside are called landscapes.

Four hundred years ago, nobody painted the countryside for its own sake. Artists used landscape in a painting only as a setting for another subject. At that time people thought that paintings should be about something or somebody in particular. They illustrated religious stories or myths, or were portraits of famous people.

Although very early landscape paintings do exist, they do not show what the countryside was really like. The ancient Greeks painted the walls of their town houses with idyllic scenes of country life. The artist imagined a scene with sheep, a shepherd, a mountain, a villa – none of which he had actually seen.

Creating depth

The next time you are in the country, look as far into the distance as you can, to the place where the land meets the sky (the horizon). Look at the colour of the scenery near to you and compare it with the colour of the land at the horizon. You will notice that the further away you look, the paler and more hazy the colours become.

For a long time, artists used the same colours at the front of their paintings (the foreground) as they did for the distance (the background). This meant that their pictures looked flat. As soon as they began to paint paler colours in the distance and stronger colours in the foreground, pictures looked more real. Changing the colours created a sense of depth and space. This technique is called aerial perspective. Look at paintings by John Constable and Grant Wood and see how they have used these techniques in their pictures.

Another way in which an artist can create depth is to draw faraway things smaller than if they were in the foreground. This is called linear perspective (see page 35).

These wall paintings were intended to be for decoration only, in much the same way as wallpaper is today.

Important landscape artists

The seventeenth-century French artist Claude Lorrain was one of the first people to take landscape painting seriously. Unlike artists before him, he went out to look at the countryside before painting a

Depth games

To create depth in a picture, the colours in the background should be paler than the colours in the foreground (see page 4). See what happens if you paint the reverse.

What you need
- paper and pencil
- paints: watercolours are best
- jars of water

What you do

1 Sketch a simple landscape.
2 Draw or trace the picture on to a separate sheet or photocopy the first one, so you have two identical versions.
3 Paint one version with the background in pale colours, the middle ground in slightly darker colours and the foreground in even darker, stronger colours.

4 Paint the second picture with the background in strong, dark colours, the middle ground in slightly paler colours and the foreground in very pale, washed-out colours.
5 Compare your two pictures. Does one look right and the other wrong? Which one stretches into the distance?

picture. He was particularly keen to capture the way the light changes at dawn and dusk and how this affects the appearance of the landscape.

Although he did observe nature, Claude's paintings are still not true representations of the countryside. He ignored unpleasant, ugly things and concentrated on creating a feeling of harmony. His paintings have a strangely peaceful atmosphere. Claude was a very influential artist. Some rich people landscaped their gardens to look like his pictures.

While Claude was painting in Italy and in France, Dutch artists were also painting landscapes. The

Visit an art gallery where you can see Impressionist paintings, or look in the library for a book on the Impressionists. You will see that the pictures are made up of many separate blobs of colour that don't make much sense close-to. If you gradually step further back, the picture will start to fall into place. Compare a picture by Paul Cézanne with one by Claude Monet or Camille Pissarro. What differences can you see?

artists Jan Van Goyen and Jacob van Ruïsdael were among the most popular seventeenth-century Dutch landscape painters. They painted realistic pictures of the Dutch countryside. Unlike Claude's tranquil, golden paintings, the sky in their pictures is often overcast and the trees are blown about by the wind, just as they are in real life.

John Constable, a nineteenth-century English landscape painter, also filled his pictures with gusty winds and troubled skies. Although he admired the work of Claude, Constable believed that landscape painting should be true to life. He included everything he saw in his pictures, whether they were considered unpleasant or not.

Constable loved the shapes of clouds. He painted the way they are affected by wind and light. It is very hard to paint clouds, because they

▲ Although there are figures in this painting, the real subject is the landscape. See how small the people are compared to the trees and buildings. The artist has used aerial perspective: the background is painted in much paler colours than the foreground. [The Father of Psyche Sacrificing at the Temple of Apollo, Claude Lorrain]

change and move so quickly. Constable drew many quick sketches outdoors and then painted what he had recorded in his studio.

Painting with light

In the nineteenth century, a group of French artists completely changed the art of landscape painting. They were less concerned with painting an accurate record of nature. Instead they wanted to capture an impression of what they saw. They were called the Impressionists.

The Impressionists, among them Claude Monet and Camille Pissarro (see pages 8 and 13), experimented with the way light and shadow alter the way things look. Their paintings have very few lines. They are made up of splashes of colour straight from the tube, rather than colours first mixed on a palette. They dabbed the paint on with small brushstrokes, building up layers of flickering colour.

Many artists in France and elsewhere admired the

▼ John Constable, who painted this picture, liked painting realistic landscapes. He made many sketches of clouds, trees, the reflection of light on water, to make sure they looked right in his paintings. Look at the sky in this picture. The clouds are made up of different colours (cream, grey, blue) and different shapes, just like they are in real life.
[Dedham Lock and Mill, *John Constable*]

◄ *This is a picture of a garden. The leaves on the trees and the flowers have been painted very loosely with dabs of paint, but they are still recognizable. The artist wanted to create an impression of what he saw rather than a perfect copy. What time of year do you think it is? Can you identify the purple flowers?*
[The Artist's Garden at Giverny, *Claude Monet*]

Impressionists and copied their style. A group of American artists went to Giverny, where Monet lived, to learn his technique. In Giverny today there is a museum devoted to the American Impressionists. The most famous is Mary Cassatt, who lived in Paris for most of her life and exhibited with the French Impressionists there.

The French artist Paul Cézanne took Impressionism one step further. He believed that everything in nature is based on three shapes: the cone, the sphere and the cylinder. By stressing these forms with dark outlines and solid blocks of colour, he made Impressionism more solid and less light and airy.

The colour of landscape

Every country has different scenery, and even within each country the landscape changes according to the region. These differences affect the colours that artists use to paint the landscape, and also their techniques.

China, with its amazing mountains and cascading waterfalls, lends itself to the fluid medium of watercolour. African painters capture the country's heat and vastness

An Impressionist for the day

Paint a picture using small splashes of paint, like Monet. Don't be tempted to use longer brushstrokes: if you do the picture won't be nearly so effective.

What you need
- paper and pencil
- poster paints
- brushes
- jars of water

What you do
1 Draw the shape of your picture with a pencil on a piece of paper. Try a flower or a tree instead of a landscape if you prefer.

2 Dab the paint on in small blobs. Do not paint in any lines and do not paint solid blocks of colour. The whole picture should consist of splashes of different colours.

3 When the painting is dry, stick it up on a wall. Stand back and look at it from a distance. What is the dominant colour in your picture?

▼ *Where do you think the artist was standing when he painted this picture? We can easily recognize everything in the picture because the artist has used simple shapes and strong colours. Compare one of the trees here with one of Constable's trees. [Stone City,* Grant Wood]

with warm brown and orange. An artist painting the falling leaves in New England, in the United States, would use quite different colours from an artist painting the hot, southern states in the heat of summer. What colours would you use to paint the countryside near you? What kind of brushstrokes would you use: short, lively ones or long, peaceful ones?

The modern landscape

There are no longer any rules about what is a good and what is a bad subject for a painting, and modern artists paint in many different styles. They may paint very realistic pictures, where every blade of grass is shown clearly, or they may choose to do an abstract picture, in which a few brushstrokes in certain colours suggest a whole landscape.

Why not paint your favourite bit of countryside? Try doing a realistic version and an abstract version of the same scene.

 # Towns and cities

City life

Cities are lively places, full of all kinds of people, buildings, traffic and activities. They are constantly changing. Old buildings are knocked down and new ones built.

Cities are full of contrasts. Next to an old Gothic church you might find a massive, 100-storey tower block. A tramp may be asleep in the doorway of an expensive hotel. A street that is crowded by day is empty at night.

Cities are often frightening, too – so many people, so much noise and so much crime.

These are all reasons why artists like to paint cities. There is such a lot going on, so much movement, so many subjects for paintings.

Town versus country

Painting a city is quite different from painting a landscape. The countryside is made up of soft lines, curved shapes and few people. The city is full of tall, straight buildings and people and cars.

A palette for the city and the country

The colours an artist uses is called his or her palette (after the hand-held board on which the artist mixes paints). The palette used for a city painting is very different from that which is used in landscape painting. Try this experiment.

What you need
- a painting of a city and another of a landscape
- pencil and paper
- watercolour paints
- brushes
- jars of water

What you do

1 Look at one of the city pictures in this chapter and compare it with a landscape painting (there are some in Chapter 1). Or find two other pictures to compare.
2 On your sheet of paper, write down the colours you can see in the city painting. Be as accurate as you can: describe the blue or grey or black carefully (for example, 'light blue', 'slate blue, 'green-grey', 'dull black').

3 Next to the name of each colour, try to match it exactly by mixing up your paints and dabbing colour on your paper until you get it right. When you have matched them all, you have your city palette.
4 Repeat the exercise for your landscape painting.
5 Notice how your colour descriptions and your finished palette for each picture differ.

The country stretches far away into the distance. You cannot see very far in the city, because your view is blocked by buildings and walls.

The colours of the countryside are greens, browns and blues. Cities are often darker: you will see greys and blacks with splashes of yellow and white from neon lights and car headlights, and brighter colours in shop windows and advertisements.

The first cities

As long as cities have existed, artists have painted them. However, unlike landscapes, they were seldom the sole subject of a painting. They were used as settings for stories from the Bible or other religious books.

Long ago, artists did not go out into cities with a sketchbook and draw what they saw there. They painted from memory or from their imaginations. As a result,

many of the buildings they painted look out of proportion and to the wrong scale.

City people

As cities grew bigger, more people came to live and work in them. Going to market, walking by the river, working in an office, sitting and talking on a park bench – all these activities added interest to the city scene.

Many artists in the nineteenth century were attracted to Paris. Edgar Degas and Edouard Manet painted realistic pictures of people going about their lives against the backdrop of the city. The Impressionist Camille Pissarro also went

▼ This is just one part of a very long wall painting that shows what an Italian city looked like 600 years ago. There is much to look at in the picture. See if you can find: some builders; a shop; and at least three different shapes of windows. The city is surrounded by a wall to keep it safe from attack. How else does it differ from a modern city? [Good Government in the City, *Ambrogio Lorenzetti*]

there to paint. Although he was a country-lover at heart, Pissarro painted many city scenes in later life. There was a practical reason for this: he had had an eye operation and was advised by doctors to stay indoors. Used to getting up at 5 am to paint landscapes and unable to bear the thought of not working, he had an idea. He could rent rooms in a city and paint what he saw out of the windows. This explains why so many of Pissarro's city pictures are painted from a high point.

Shiny new cities

In the 1920s, when modern building materials such as concrete and steel were introduced, cities began to change. In some places, new buildings reached high into the sky. The cities of the future would look very different from those of the past.

Fernand Léger was a French artist who wanted to capture the excitement of the new industrial age. His paintings, with their bright colours and movement, glorify the modern city. They show all the good things about it and ignore the less pleasant aspects. His factories

City by night collage

Cities change at night. Electric light shining out from windows, neon signs and car headlights take the place of natural light. Long shadows form, and tall buildings loom in the darkness.

What you need
- large piece of paper
- paints
- paintbrush
- black, grey and yellow paper
- silver foil

What you do

1 First of all, paint stripes of night-sky colour across the piece of paper. Start at the bottom and work up. Paint a stripe of dark orange, one of light orange and another one of yellow. Paint the next stripe light blue and the final one a darker blue.

2 Cut out squares and rectangles from the grey and black paper. These will be your buildings. Make some tall and thin like tower blocks, others short and squat like factories. Glue the buildings on to the bottom of your night sky.

3 Cut out some small squares and rectangles from the yellow paper. Glue these to the buildings to represent windows and doors.

4 Cut moon and star shapes out of the silver foil and glue them on to the sky. If you like, add neon signs in bright colours.

► *Camille Pissarro who painted this street scene, was one of a group of artists called the Impressionists (see page 7). If you look at the picture closely, you will see that it is made up of small dashes of colour. By looking at the length of the shadows and the colour of the pavement and the buildings, can you tell whether it is morning or afternoon?*
[*Paris Street Scene, Camille Pissarro*]

Architectural features

Start looking carefully at buildings and notice how many of them have been designed with interesting doors, windows and other features. The decorations on old buildings are very different from those on modern buildings. Which are more elaborate?

What you need
- sketchbook, or clipboard and sheets of paper
- pencils or coloured pens
- a fold-up, portable seat might be useful

What you do
Draw a selection of architectural details in your sketchbook. Keep a page for windows, a page for doors, a page for railings and so on. Collect as many different kinds as you can.

Here are some features to look out for (you will find plenty of others):
- gargoyles (grotesque faces near the roof on churches and other old buildings)
- towers and spires

- pillars with a decorative capital (a capital is found on the top of the pillar – see page 23)
- bridges • chimneys • weather vanes
- arches • windows and doors • clocks
- brickwork patterns • iron railings

are bright, attractive, friendly places, unlike the grim reality of many of them.

Soon people began to realize that these new cities were not as wonderful as they had hoped. Poverty did not disappear. If anything, it was worse. Cities had grown more congested and people were isolated from one another in the new, high blocks of flats.

Artists such as Edward Burra began to paint this grim side of city life – poor people, criminals and prostitutes. The buildings in his paintings look shabby and slightly derelict.

Do you live in or near a city? When you are next out and about, or when you visit a city, look carefully at the colours you see. Look at the streets, the buildings, the shop signs, the people and the traffic, and make a list of the colours you would use to paint your city.

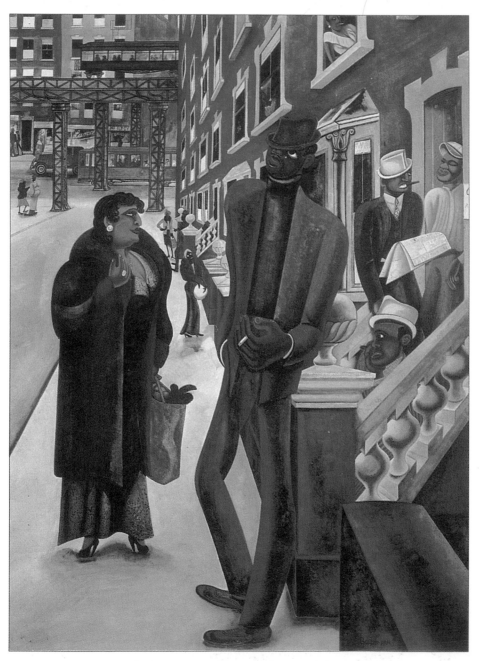

◀ *The people in this picture, which was painted in the 1920s, are in an area of New York called Harlem. Can you imagine what the lives of the people in the picture were like? For clues, look at their clothes and the way they are standing. The artist did not paint exactly what he saw. He exaggerated people's movements and expressions to create stronger characters. All the horizontal lines in this picture get closer together in the distance. This technique of creating depth is called linear perspective (see page 35).*
[Harlem, *Edward Burra*]

Pictures in the air

Many large buildings in cities have boards with huge advertisements on them. These are called hoardings or billboards. The pictures on them are designed to catch the attention of people on the move. The image has to be strong to make passers-by notice it. Usually, the picture has been printed on paper and pasted on the wall but occasionally it has been painted by an artist on the spot.

▶ This picture was painted in 1938. If the artist painted the same scene today, it would look quite different. The road would be full of cars, there would be no smoke coming out of the chimneys and very few people would be wearing hats. Look at the figures in the picture. Notice how they get smaller the further away they are. Can you paint a figure or a dog like those in the painting?
[Street Scene, Berwick-upon-Tweed, L.S. Lowry]

The industrial city

L.S. Lowry, an English painter, combined two different aspects of city life – its gaiety and its poverty. He painted the streets and factories of his home town of Salford and other cities in the north of England.

In his paintings, people come and go, talk to each other, play games and go to work. Yet his pictures do not portray a bright, modern city. He painted in dark, sombre colours and included tall chimneys belching dirty, black smoke over dingy, narrow streets. His scenes are often full of 'matchstick' people trudging reluctantly to work or wearily home again.

The sea and the seaside

The sea is vast, and always changing. It looks and feels different according to the climate and the coastline of a particular country. A picturesque, sandy beach has a different atmosphere from a rocky shore with steep cliffs and foaming breakers. The sea may be calm or violent, sunny blue or stormy green, warm and balmy or freezing cold, peaceful or dangerous.

The sea conjures up many different feelings: happiness, peace, excitement and fear. Because of this, and because of all the activities that happen on and by the sea, it is a perfect subject for artists.

Early times

Pictures of the sea are relatively modern, but there are some exceptions. Early illustrated manuscripts showed scenes from the story of Noah's Ark. This was a splendid subject for a painting. Artists could paint the building of the ark, the animals entering it, the long days at sea and the safe landing of the ark when the water level finally went back to normal.

Many fourteenth- and fifteenth-century artists illustrated episodes from the life of Jesus. Some of these show Jesus walking on the

▼ *In this Japanese print, a Buddhist saint called Nichiren is calming the wild sea by speaking some special words. The storm has been whipped up by an evil spirit. Look at how the artist has drawn the waves; in some ways they look more like plants than the sea. Notice how terrified the sailors look, especially when compared with the calm Nichiren.* [Nichiren Calming the Storm with an Invocation, *Yoshimory*]

▲ *Do you think the people in this picture are hot or cold? The sun is out and they are sitting in the shade under umbrellas, but look at the clouds and the way clothes are being blown about. The composition of this picture is divided into three parts. Where do the boundaries of each part lie?*
[*At the Seaside, William Merritt Chase*]

water, or St Peter fishing. The artists were more concerned with telling the story than painting the sea accurately. They painted the water in a stylized, unrealistic way, making it look calm and undisturbed. There is little movement – only the occasional ripple.

Some ancient wall paintings illustrate scenes from the story of Odysseus, a Greek hero who had many adventures. In these pictures the sea is painted simply with horizontal brushstrokes and looks calm and flat, even though the stories often describe stormy, violent seas.

The Greek poet Homer sometimes described the sea as 'wine dark', which gives a hint of menace and fear.

Beside the seaside

The seaside was not always a popular place to spend weekends and holidays. It was only in the nineteenth century that people started to go to the seaside to swim and relax. Many artists of the time enjoyed depicting this new activity. People lie in the sun, play games and swim in the sea. Nothing important happens. An atmosphere of lazy warmth and pleasure fills each picture.

17

Beach sculpture

The next time you go to the seaside, look for unusual-looking pebbles, shells and pieces of driftwood. Make a sculpture out of them.

What you need
- collecting box or bag
- shells, pebbles, fossils, pieces of wood or chalk, buffeted by the sea into interesting shapes

What you do

1 Arrange your collection in a pattern on a flat surface. Take out anything that does not look interesting.
2 Does your arrangement remind you of anything? A figure? An animal? A monster? Keep arranging the shapes until you come up with something you like. Then glue the shapes together with strong glue to make a sculpture.

▼ *Can you see the boat in this painting? If you look closely, you can see the sail. The real subject of the picture is not the boat, however, but the sea. Look how wild it is. The artist, Turner, wanted people who saw this painting to feel small in the face of the hugeness of nature. What is unusual about the colours he has used?* [Rough Sea, J.M.W. Turner]

Turner and the sea

Turner was particularly interested in capturing the wilder side of nature and was famous for his paintings of stormy seas. In some pictures the subject of the painting (usually a ship) is almost lost among the great swirling brushstrokes that represent waves, clouds and wind.

To achieve his special effects, Turner invented a new way of painting. First he put layers of paint on to his canvas and then he dragged another, usually paler, colour over them with a brush to create a rough effect. Sometimes he put the paint on with a knife for extra thickness.

Wild and romantic

In the eighteenth and nineteenth centuries, before there were aeroplanes, many people travelled by ship. Instruments for navigation were less sophisticated than they are now and many ships were wrecked, particularly along the coast. Artists who were rather bored by beach scenes loved the drama of these events. They enjoyed painting storms, shipwrecks and the heroic deeds that accompanied them. These artists were called Romantics.

The Romantics, including Eugène Delacroix and Jean Auguste Dominique Ingres in France, and Joseph Turner in England, did not paint in a similar style. But they all painted pictures showing turbulent feelings and strong passions. They wanted their pictures to stir the emotions of those who looked at them.

Sea-painting techniques

The technique for painting a stormy sea is different from that for a calm sea. The sea in a beach scene is flat. The artist might paint it loosely with washes of watercolour in horizontal lines. Rough seas are dangerous and hostile. The artist usually paints them with swirls of thick paint that rear up over the rocks, ships and figures.

Oil paint is useful for painting stormy seas because it can be laid on thickly. Artists sometimes put it on so thickly that the surface of the picture is bumpy.

To create a feeling of movement and fear, artists show ships and figures blown about by the wind, and dark, menacing clouds. All the ingredients of the picture combine to create a scene of tragedy and disaster.

Painting the sea

Look at the different sorts of seas in the pictures in this chapter. Rough seas require a different painting technique from calm seas.

What you need
- pencil and paper   • brushes   • jar of water
- paints: watercolours or oils (oils are better for stormy seas, but they are more difficult to use)

What you do
First draw two similar pictures showing the coast, the sea and a boat.

Rough sea
1 Draw the shapes of the waves with a pencil. Make them swell up high in the air. Draw lots of them.
2 Paint the waves using dark blues and greens. Use thick, sweeping brushstrokes. Paint your brushstrokes in the direction in which the water is moving.
3 Add white paint at the tips of the waves or anywhere else you think surf might form.
4 Paint your boat at an angle in the waves.
5 Make the sky cloudy and angry looking.

Calm sea
1 Paint the sea first. Choose a light blue or green and paint it on smoothly with horizontal strokes.
2 Add another shade of blue or green to make it more realistic – the sea is never just one colour, but different shades of blues and greens. The sun also shines on the sea, so add some splashes of yellow or orange on the water.
3 Add a boat. In a calm sea your boat will be reflected in the water.
4 The sky is reflected in the sea. Any clouds make shadows on the water.

Look at some sea pictures. Notice whether they are 'warm' or 'cold'. Seaside pictures are usually warm, stormy pictures cold. The best way for an artist to create a sense of warmth or cold is with colour. Yellows, oranges and reds make us think of heat, whereas blues, greys and greens are cold colours. Look at the paintings in this chapter. See what makes some feel warm and some feel cold.

▼ *This painting shows a scene on the River Thames. You can tell it is in London because you can see Tower Bridge in the background. The artist, André Derain, liked to use large areas of plain colour. Sometimes his choice of colour was quite unusual. Have you ever seen a green sky, or green and orange water? Do you think it matters that his colours aren't realistic?* [Pool of London, André Derain]

Arrival and departure

Ports and harbours have always been popular subjects for paintings. Claude Lorrain (see Chapter 1) painted huge ships setting sail in the golden sunlight. André Derain, a twentieth-century French artist, painted brightly coloured, busy ports, and Georges Seurat, a Frenchman who applied isolated dots of colour to vast canvases, liked to paint boats floating in sunny harbours.

Building a place

Every building, from a railway shed to the most spectacular palace, has been specially designed. Your home has. So has your school. A person who designs buildings is called an architect.

Architects influence our lives. Together with planners, they decide the shapes of our homes and how they look. They decide whether a skyscraper should be 20 or 30 storeys high, or more. They design your local library and theatre, for example.

Ancient buildings

There have been architects for thousands of years. They designed the buildings of ancient Greece and Rome. We may not know their names now, but we know what their buildings looked like, because the ruins still exist.

The Parthenon, a huge ancient Greek temple, can still be seen today in Athens. It is an impressive sight, a huge white stone ruin standing on a hill overlooking the city, but it was even more splendid when

▲ *The Parthenon is an ancient Greek temple which overlooks the city of Athens. It is built of white marble. The architects who designed it were called Ictinus and Callicrates and it was built in 448-42 BC. Originally it was adorned with sculpture but this was removed in 1801-03 by Lord Elgin (the sculpture is now in the British Museum). The architecture is in the Doric order (see the information box on page 23).*
[The Parthenon, Athens, *Johan Wolfensberger*]

The classical orders of architecture

There were three major types – or orders – of architecture in ancient Greece and Rome. You can tell which is which by looking at the capitals of pillars on the buildings. The three orders were:

Ionic: the capital was in the shape of a pair of ram's horns
Doric: the capital was plain and undecorated
Corinthian: the capital was carved in the shape of the leaves of the acanthus plant.

it was first built. In those days it contained colourful sculptures and mosaics of gods and goddesses and heroes at war. They were all painted in bright colours.

Places of prayer

Some of the most spectacular buildings are places of worship. They are important places where people worship their gods, so religious authorities spend time and money to make them special.

Mosques are where Muslims worship. The design of mosques is based on the prophet Muhammad's house. Muhammad built a raised platform outside his home. From here he spoke to the people who gathered to hear him speak. Architects included a raised platform in the first mosques. Later, the platforms developed into towers, called minarets. Five times each day an official,

▶ *This building in Istanbul, Turkey, is almost 400 years old. It is usually called the Blue Mosque but its correct name is the Mosque of Ahmed I. It is made up of a series of domes of different sizes. The towers at the sides are minarets from which the faithful are called to prayer. Compare this mosque with the Gothic cathedral on page 24.*

called a muezzin, stands on a minaret and calls the people to say their prayers.

One of the most famous mosques in the world is the Mosque of Ahmed I, or the Blue Mosque, in Istanbul, Turkey. It is a huge, dramatic building, with six minarets and a series of domes.

Types of architecture

The earliest Christian buildings were simple, rectangular rooms, large enough for a number of people to gather. Gradually, churches and cathedrals became more grand.

Different styles of architecture have special names. Many early cathedrals were built in the Gothic style. Gothic architects wanted to create buildings filled with light and space, something as close to heaven as possible. Their buildings are tall and often have pointed, stained glass windows and arches reaching up to God.

Later architects, such as Christopher Wren, who designed St Paul's Cathedral, London, were interested in classical architecture – the buildings of ancient Greece

▲ *Being inside this cathedral in Exeter, England, is rather like being in a forest. The architect has created this feeling by using many vertical lines and by constructing soaring vaults (the arches that form the ceiling) that meet in the middle like the branches of trees. This type of architecture, called Gothic, was popular in the Middle Ages.*

and Rome. Like classical buildings, those designed by Wren are imposing and simple, and on a large scale.

Baroque architecture is very decorative. St Peter's Basilica in Rome is a good example. Inside, Gian Lorenzo Bernini decorated it with twisting columns and elaborate sculpture that included gold sun-rays and angels sitting on clouds. Outside he built a huge oval area surrounded by columns.

The ruins of great classical buildings have always inspired architects. When you are in a town or city, see if you can spot columns that look like those on page 23.

Modern buildings

▼ *In the 1970s, a type of architecture called Hi-tech was popular. The Pompidou Centre in Paris, France, is one example. Instead of putting water pipes, electricity cables and lifts inside the building, the architects, Richard Rogers and Rinzo Piano, put them on the outside. This leaves more room inside. The building is brightly coloured with many of the cables coated in red and green plastic.*

At the beginning of this century, architects wanted to get away from old ideas and build useful buildings that looked original. Le Corbusier was an architect who saw buildings as machines to live in rather than places of beauty. His ideas led to the construction of high-rise blocks of flats. These tower blocks are simple shapes and have no decoration on them. Le Corbusier designed whole cities based on squares and rectangles. This architectural style is called Modernist.

Reacting against tower blocks, Post-Modernist architects use a variety of building materials and styles. They still design tall buildings, but give them more interesting features than Modernist versions. Post-Modernist buildings are more likely to be shocking or at least surprising.

The Hi-tech Pompidou Centre in Paris, France, was controversial when it was built in 1977. People still have strong opinions about it: some find it artistic and attractive; to others it is an eyesore.

Practical design

Each country has its own type of architecture that takes into account practical considerations as well as traditional design.

If the climate is hot, buildings are designed to keep out the sun. They have small windows and are often painted white to reflect the heat. If it is cold, it is important that homes have thick walls, and roofs that slope so that rain and snow will slide off.

The materials available also influence building design. In the Rocky Mountains in the United States, for example, log cabins are popular because of the number of trees there. In big American cities, however, the most widely used material is reinforced concrete.

The amount of land available also influences building style. Skyscrapers look dramatic but they have a practical purpose, too. They hold many people but take up little space on the ground.

The American architect Frank Lloyd Wright believed that it was the rooms inside a building that really mattered, not its appearance on the outside. Nevertheless, his

Building materials

Until the nineteenth century, most buildings were made of natural materials such as stone, wood, mud and slate.

Early Gothic cathedrals had stone walls – which had to be thick enough to support the height of the building – and vaulted stone ceilings. Later Gothic buildings had thinner walls and were supported on the outside by complicated stone structures called buttresses.

In the nineteenth century, architects began to use cast iron in buildings. This made them lighter than buildings made of solid stone. The Eiffel Tower in Paris is made of cast iron.

Buildings constructed with steel and glass are even lighter and higher. Some constructions, such as the Crystal Palace in London, were built completely of iron and glass.

Skyscrapers are made of cubes of steel frames piled one on top of the other. The weight in these tower blocks is not taken by the walls but is evenly spread through each box.

buildings are far from boring to look at. The Guggenheim Museum in New York, USA, for example, is a very unusual shape as well as being popular with most people who see it.

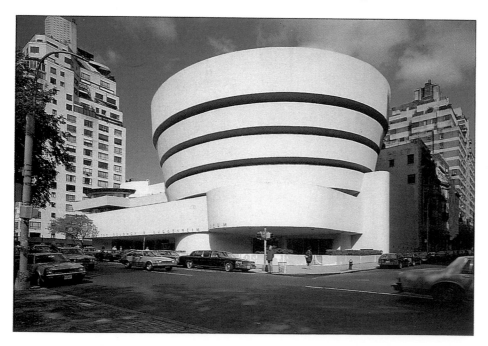

◀ *From the outside, the Guggenheim Museum, designed by Frank Lloyd Wright, looks as though it is made of four circular discs placed one on top of the other. As you enter the building, you realize that it is really a huge spiral. You walk up through the building, looking at paintings as you go, on a ramp that spirals right to the top. Does the shape of the building remind you of anything?*

The exotic east

In China, traditional buildings are made of wood on a stone foundation. Many roofs have tiles with turned-up edges (purely for decorative effect). Often houses are constructed around a central courtyard and are only one storey high.

Traditional Japanese buildings were also made of wood. In Japan, a house and its garden or surroundings are designed so that they blend together in harmony. Some gardens not only have plants but large stones and pebbles arranged in attractive shapes. Modern Japanese buildings are just as exciting as those in the United States, but they often contain traditional features such as sliding paper screens for walls, and rush matting on the floor. There is very little furniture.

A fabulous palace

Make your own small-scale spectacular building, full of interesting detail.

What you need
- a variety of household objects (make sure nobody needs them!). Use empty cereal boxes, toilet-paper rolls, milk-bottle tops, spherical washing-powder containers (for making domes), straws, empty matchboxes, and so on.
- glue
- scissors
- paint (gold and silver paint are useful)

What you do
1 Assemble your raw materials. Experiment with making different types of structures. Don't glue anything together yet.
2 When you are happy with your palace, start gluing. Begin with the basic structure and then add all the more elaborate, decorative parts.
3 Paint your palace using bright paint and exotic detail.

A place to dream

Piero di Cosimo, an early Italian artist, used to stare at the stains on a wall and the clouds in the sky. In the shapes they created, he thought he could see processions of people, amazing cities and strange landscapes. He used what he saw in his head as inspiration for his paintings.

Do you ever see pictures of people or animals in the shapes of clouds? Or in the trees? In the flames of a fire? Or the shadows on the wall? If so, you have used your imagination to conjure up pictures, just as Piero di Cosimo did. Many artists find they prefer to use their imaginations for inspiration rather than the real world of landscapes, portraits or historical events.

Doorways to other worlds

Hieronymus Bosch, a fifteenth-century artist, painted strange pictures illustrating passages from the Bible. He invented dragons with wheels, living rocks,

Rousseau, the naïve artist
Henri 'Le Douanier' Rousseau is known as a naïve artist, because he had no formal art teaching. The word naïve means innocent or unsophisticated.

Rousseau began painting when he retired from his job as a customs official (*douanier* is the French for customs official). He taught himself to paint by copying paintings in the Louvre, the great art gallery in Paris. The subjects of his paintings are often exotic and include snake charmers, gypsies and tropical jungles. His work is very powerful and was much admired by other artists of his time, including Pablo Picasso.

▲ *Henri Rousseau never saw a jungle – he painted this picture from his imagination. Its original title was* Surprise. *Why?* [Tropical Storm with a Tiger (Surprise), *Henri Rousseau*]

▶ *The central figures in this picture are Adam, Eve and God, but what are all those creatures around them? Some are familiar but the others are very odd. Look at the mountains, and at the fountain in the centre. Have you ever seen anything like them before?* [The Garden of Earthly Delights, *Hieronymus Bosch*]

weird vegetables, huge knife-wielding ears and birds wearing jackets. Although he lived long ago, his work still influences artists today.

Several other artists, such as Gustave Moreau, Odilon Redon and Henri Rousseau, preferred to paint from their imaginations rather than from real life. They created an imaginary world into which we can all escape. Moreau took stories from the Bible and myths, and set them in a world he had invented.

Dreams and the Surrealists

At the beginning of the twentieth century, a group of artists called the Surrealists caused quite a stir with their extraordinary paintings. *Surrealism* is a French word which means 'more than real'. Surrealist painters stopped planning their pictures and painted freely, as children do. They let their brushes fly with their imaginations.

Salvador Dali, Joan Miró, Marc Chagall and Max Ernst are all important Surrealist painters who used their imaginations in their paintings. They also took inspiration from their dreams.

The meanings of dreams

The Surrealists were influenced by Sigmund Freud, the first person to use psychoanalysis. Psychoanalysts help people discover what lies in their unconscious minds. The unconscious mind is full of memories, emotions and ideas, but it lies buried beneath the conscious mind, which we use every day to learn, talk and play. Freud thought that the best way to discover what lies in the unconscious mind was to study dreams.

Do you remember your dreams? We tend to forget most of them, but those we do remember are full of strange and unlikely things. In some dreams we may fly over a country we have never been to, or a cat may change into a coffee cup and back again.

▲ *At first, this landscape looks fairly normal. The plants are a bit strange, but believable. Then, as we look closer, we find all kinds of peculiar things lurking in the undergrowth. Look at the red figure with a bird's head. What other creatures can you see? The picture is called* Evening Song, *which sounds peaceful. Do you think it is peaceful?* [Evening Song, *Max Ernst*]

▼ *You may find it difficult at first to work out what is happening in this picture. But if you look closely you will see figures and buildings. It is one of a series of paintings called 'nocturnes' by the artist James Whistler. It shows a night-time scene in London. Whistler tried using different techniques to capture the effects of light, especially at night.* [Nocturne in Black and Gold, *James Whistler*]

Dream diary

It is not easy to remember your dreams, because they seem to fade away as soon as you wake up. But you can train yourself to remember enough to paint a picture.

What you need
- pencil
- notepad
- felt tips or pastels
- paints, brushes and paper

What you do
1 Every morning for a week, as soon as you wake up, sketch images from your dreams the night before. Do not try to create a complete scene, just the impressions and incidents that were particularly vivid.

2 At the end of the week, look through your sketches and choose something to make into a larger painting.

3 Show it to your friends. What do they think your dreams might mean?

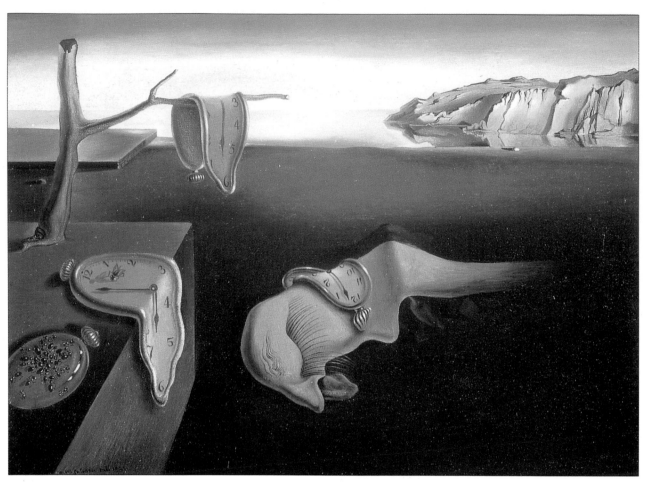

The odd thing is that at the time of the dream we consider these things to be quite normal. Put these things into a painting, however, as the Surrealists did, and they do not look normal at all.

Dali's dream paintings

Salvador Dali painted peculiar dream images. He called his paintings 'hand-painted dream photographs'. Dali painted his dreams in a very realistic, almost photographic way, and yet they contain

How do you react to the pictures in this chapter? Do they excite you or do they make you feel uncomfortable? Try to think why they have that effect.

very unreal objects. He would take a familiar object and make it do something it could not possibly do in real life. For example, he painted a watch that was so soft it melted over a wall. His pictures are disturbing because they make the impossible look normal.

▲ *This painting is a mixture of the familiar and the strange. The beach is based on a real one in France and looks normal. In contrast, the central image is very odd. We recognize the watches, but at the same time know that really they aren't soft and wouldn't droop like they do here. Even more confusingly, the picture is painted to look almost like a photograph. We are left feeling that such a peculiar landscape might just exist. [The Persistence of Memory (1931), Salvador Dali]*

Visit the future

You have probably seen a film about the future, or read a science-fiction book or comic. How do you see the future yourself? As something bleak and horrifying like a bad dream? As a world full of extraordinary colours or weird creatures?

What you need
- pencil and large piece of paper
- paints – you might like to try spray paints for extra effect
- brushes
- jar of water
- your imagination

What you do

1 Use a large piece of paper, so that your picture is especially effective.

2 Sketch out your landscape of the future. Invent strange-shaped trees and rocks, odd creatures and a strange atmosphere.

3 Remember the rules of landscape mentioned on page 4. To be effective, the background, middle ground and foreground of your picture should be painted according to these rules.

4 On the other hand, try and forget everything else you know about ordinary landscape. The grass of the future may not be green, animals may not have four legs, or even look like animals, the sky may not be blue, the sun could be purple, square and huge rather than yellow and round.

6 No place like home

When you visit your friends or relatives, do you like to have a good look around their home? We are all curious about other people's lives: how they decorate their rooms, what kind of objects they like to display, what colours they like. A person's home is a reflection of their personality. That is one reason why artists like to paint interiors. But collections of household objects, the patterns on curtains or carpets, how the light changes the atmosphere of a room – all these, too, make wonderful subjects for a painting.

The Master of Flémalle

Interiors have not always been popular. It was the Dutch who started the trend for painting everyday life and

▶ Although this is a religious scene showing Saint Barbara, the artist has chosen to set it in a domestic interior. He has recorded everything in the room in great detail. The view through the window shows Saint Barbara's symbol – the tower. She was kept in a tower by her father because she was so beautiful.
[Saint Barbara, Robert Campin, the Master of Flémalle]

Pictures in perspective

Draw a railway track that seems to stretch back into the distance.

What you need
- ruler
- pencil
- paper
- crayons, coloured pencils or felt-tip pens

What you do
1 Mark your vanishing point (see page 35) on the horizon line.
2 Draw two lines that widen out from the dot to the bottom of your paper. That's your railway track in perspective. Then draw some lines in pencil to help you position some objects.
3 Add trees, bushes, telegraph poles, railway sleepers (the pieces of wood between the tracks), all in perspective along your pencil lines.
4 Paint your picture and rub out any pencil lines you no longer need.

Linear perspective

To make their pictures more realistic and to create an illusion of depth, artists use perspective. They can do this with colour (see aerial perspective in the 'Creating depth' box on page 4) or with lines – linear perspective.

To get linear perspective right, you have to make sure that lines in a picture get closer together the further away they go, until they eventually meet. The place where they meet is called the vanishing point. You paint distant objects smaller than those in the foreground. Look at the painting of Vincent Van Gogh's bedroom on page 37. Notice how the chair at the back of the room is smaller than the one at the front.

the homes of ordinary people. Robert Campin, also known as the Master of Flémalle, lived in the Netherlands in the fifteenth century. He was one of the first artists to paint realistic interiors. Although his paintings were religious, Campin put his figures in everyday settings and the domestic details tell us all manner of things about life at that time.

Robert Campin was one of the first artists to grapple with linear perspective (see above). Before his time, figures and objects in paintings seemed to float around in space. You could not tell what was supposed to be at the front or in the background of the picture. Campin painted objects in the distance smaller than those in front, making his pictures more realistic and easier to understand than earlier ones.

Dutch homes

Jan Vermeer and Pieter de Hooch were also Dutch, but they lived 200 years after Campin. They also created a sense of perspective. Their paintings, showing people chatting in courtyards, sewing and cooking, appealed to the wealthy townspeople of the time. You can almost feel the warmth of the fire and smell the polish on the furniture when you 'enter' these pictures.

These Dutch interiors are rather like photographs, because they are an accurate record of life in one place at a particular time. If a film director wanted to make a film about the Netherlands in the seventeenth century, he could look at Vermeer's paintings and see immediately how to build a realistic set.

Still life

A picture of objects around the house – jugs, bowls of fruit, loaves of bread, books – is known as a still life. Still lifes give you practice in observing and drawing details accurately.

What you need
- a simple collection of objects on a table with a patterned tablecloth
- paints, pastels or charcoal
- paper or sketchbook

What you do

1 Arrange your objects in a pleasing composition.
2 Sketch your picture first. Circular bowls and jugs are difficult to draw accurately. Don't worry too much about this. If one object is particularly difficult, replace it with another one, or do a few practice sketches on separate pieces of paper.

3 Look carefully at the reflections in glass, how the sunlight or a lamp casts shadows on your composition, how fruit has a sheen to it, how the perspective works.
4 Finish your picture using paints or pastels.

▲ *Although there is nobody in this bedroom, we can learn a little about its occupant from his belongings. He has few things – a single bed, some clothes, two chairs, a towel, a table and some paintings. Was he rich or poor, do you think? Was he married? Did he have children? See how the artist has used many sorts of brushstrokes.* [The Artist's Bedroom, *Vincent Van Gogh*]

Diary of the artist

Pierre Bonnard and Edgar Degas, both French artists, enjoyed painting domestic life and people going about everyday chores. Henri Matisse, fascinated by pattern, painted colourful, decorative pictures of the inside of his home. He often painted his wife at home, either doing ordinary things or just sitting.

Vincent Van Gogh, who painted many self-portraits, found inspiration in the most ordinary things around his home – a chair, his bedroom, his boots – and brought them to life with dancing brushstrokes and vivid colour. His paintings are intimate and full of his personality, like a diary of his life.

Interiors are still popular today. See if you can find some by Stanley Spencer or David Hockney or any other modern artist.

Paint – a potted history

The paint we buy today is very different from that used by, say, the mural painters of ancient Egypt, or early Italian artists. They had to use materials that were easily available: ground minerals, earth, plants, water and eggs.

Tempera is one of the oldest types of paint and was used mostly on panels that were coated with a thin plaster called gesso. The artist mixed his pigments with an egg which bound the mixture and resulted in a quick-drying paint that was also luminous and hard-wearing.

Oil paint is a mixture of dry pigment and vegetable oil. Unlike tempera, it is slow drying, but this makes it easier for the artist to make corrections and build up layers of colour. Oil paint can produce a variety of effects from thin films (called glazes) to thick, bumpy, finishes.

Robert Campin and other artists of his time, especially Jan van Eyck, found that oil paint was excellent for reproducing rich, velvety textures as well as clear, transparent effects. Glass jars and thick curtains in their paintings actually look as if they were made of different materials.

Acrylic paint was invented in the twentieth century. It is made from pigment bound in a synthetic resin and was first used for painting walls because it dries quickly and is clean to use. Unlike oil paint, acrylic paint can be diluted to create a paler, more translucent effect. After painting, brushes can be cleaned in water. Oil paint is only soluble in white spirit or turpentine.

Looking at pictures of different countries is the next best thing to travelling abroad. The inside of an African, an Indian, or a Japanese home is very different from an English or American living room, and can teach you a lot about other people's lives.

Look at the pictures in this chapter and compare the furniture, the clothes, the pictures on the walls. Then look again and see what techniques each artist has used. Look at the colours, the brushstrokes, the details.

How would you paint the inside of your home? Which medium (paint, print, charcoal, crayons) would you use?

▲ *In the past, houses in Japan were traditionally made of wooden panels and paper screens. The women in this picture are called geishas. Their job is to look after men by entertaining them with music, conversation and dancing. Here they are about to serve food and tea to them in the room adjoining the one we can see. Look at the beautiful clothes they are wearing. These robes are called kimonos.*
[The Tea House at Edo, *Kunishand*]

► *What can you tell about the people in this picture? We know at once that they are elderly by looking at their faces and clothes. The artist has painted their hands very large, so perhaps he is telling us that they have spent their lives working with their hands – in the fields perhaps. The framed words from a psalm on the wall behind them tell us that they are religious people. What do you think their personalities are like? Can you invent a conversation they might have?* [The Lord is my Shepherd, *Thomas Hart Benton*]

The most fantastic bedroom in the world

Design an amazing bedroom for yourself. Include everything you would like to have in it – a sunken bath, or a bed suspended from the ceiling, a huge train set around the walls, or a whole wall of television and computer screens. Perhaps you would like a fridge always stocked with ice-cream and cold drinks?

Now paint your imaginary bedroom on a large piece of paper, using the rules of linear perspective (see page 35) as far as possible.

Amazing places

Some buildings or works of art are so unusual that they take your breath away. Even pictures of these places can fill you with wonder. Such places cannot be put into any special category. They are simply proof that human beings have always needed to express themselves artistically, often on a grand scale and sometimes in exceptionally difficult circumstances.

Pyramids

The pyramids of Egypt were the tombs of the pharaohs and other important nobles of ancient Egypt. Their enormous size and unusual shape have always attracted visitors. The great pyramid is so big that five of the world's largest churches would fit inside it. The Egyptians decorated the insides of the pyramids with paintings

▲ *The Great Wall of China is the largest single construction ever made. It was begun in the third century BC to keep out nomadic invaders from the north, and was largely rebuilt in the fifteenth and sixteenth centuries AD. On average it is 9 metres high and snakes 2,400 kilometres across northern China.* [The Great Wall of China, *William Simpson*]

▶ *The Great Pyramid is the largest of all the Egyptian pyramids. For almost 5,000 years it was the tallest building in the world. It was built by pharaoh Cheops as a tomb for himself and his wife. Deep inside is a small room where the bodies of the pharaoh and his wife were placed.*

▼ *These huge heads seem to have pushed their way out of the ground like mushrooms. They were carved from a soft volcanic stone by the people of Easter Island, in Polynesia, between AD 1000 and 1600. The only tools that were available were made of stone, shell and bones. This may explain why the carving is simple. Each head has the same big nose, pursed lips, long ears and sunken eyes. There are 600 heads on the island and some weigh more than 50 tonnes.*

telling stories about the dead people, and they loaded the tombs with treasures.

The native people of Mexico the Maya – built pyramids, too, but they made them as temples rather than tombs. They often held human sacrifices on their steps. The Temple of Quetzalcoatl in Central Mexico (built in AD 100 to 600) is a fantastic mixture of sculpture and architecture. On each step of the pyramid is a series of serpents' heads alternating with faces with circular, staring eyes.

In touch with the dead

Other ancient peoples also built memorials to their dead. The natives of Easter Island in the Pacific Ocean, for example, carved enormous stone heads of their chiefs. They thought that the chiefs inherited power from the gods and would become gods themselves when they died. The people hoped their carvings would please these new gods. All the heads look similar but it is impossible to know if they resembled the people who made them.

The people of the city of Angkor in Cambodia took this idea further. When a king died and became a god, a whole temple was built in his honour alongside the temples of his ancestors.

The pharaoh Chephren built the sphinx beside the Great Pyramid in Egypt in memory of his father, Cheops. The sphinx has the body of a crouching lion but the head of a human being.

The Taj Mahal in Agra, India, was built by a Mogul emperor as a tomb for his dead wife. He wanted to build a paradise on earth in her honour. It is such a beautiful building that many people think he succeeded. The architecture and the layout of the surrounding gardens are like descriptions of paradise in the Koran (the sacred book of the Islamic faith).

Mysterious circles

Some places are so old that we have no idea why they were built. No written records exist now, so we can only guess.

Stone circles were erected over 4,000 years ago in many places in Northern Europe. A famous example is Stonehenge in the south of

Papier mâché sculpture

It is quite easy to copy one of the Easter Island heads (see page 41). Alternatively, design your own head to model.

What you need
- wire mesh
- lots of newspaper, torn into strips
- water

- wallpaper paste
- overall or apron
- poster paints
- modelling knife

What you do

1 Make the shape of your head with the wire mesh.
2 Mix the paste and water in the bucket; follow the instructions on the packet.
3 Put some strips of newspaper into the paste and make sure they are thoroughly soaked.
4 Take out one or two strips at a time and start covering your wire mesh. Overlap each strip so that there are no gaps.

5 Build up several layers until you cannot see the wire beneath the papier mâché. Pay special attention to facial features such as the eye sockets, mouth and nose.
6 Allow the head to dry thoroughly.
7 You may need to chip away with a knife to perfect your head.
8 When it is quite dry and hard, paint it.

▼ *Do you recognize this animal? It is known as the White Horse of Uffington but really it is a cross between a horse and a dragon. This is the oldest chalk-cut figure in Britain – it was probably drawn in the first century BC, but it may be even older. Nobody knows for sure why it was drawn. One theory is that it was a symbol belonging to a tribe who lived in that area. Look at how the artist has used just a few lines to draw the animal.*

England. At first glance Stonehenge seems to be a very simple construction, but the standard of masonry is very high and the positioning of the stones is precise. Some people say that by looking at the shadows cast by the stones, it is possible to work out the date according to the lunar calendar.

Hill drawings

In some chalky areas of Britain you can see enormous figures that look as if they have been drawn on the hillside. Some of the designs are very striking and look quite modern.

The figures are not actually drawings. The artist cut a design into the hillside, removing strips of turf and revealing the white chalk beneath. Nowadays the lines are painted over with special white paint to make sure that the figures are preserved. It is surprising how well you can see the figures from a distance. The white lines show up very clearly against the green grass.

These figures, of giants, horses and dragons, are very old. Because they are so big and on high ground, some people think that they were signals to space travellers, but no one really knows if they had a purpose or were purely for decoration.

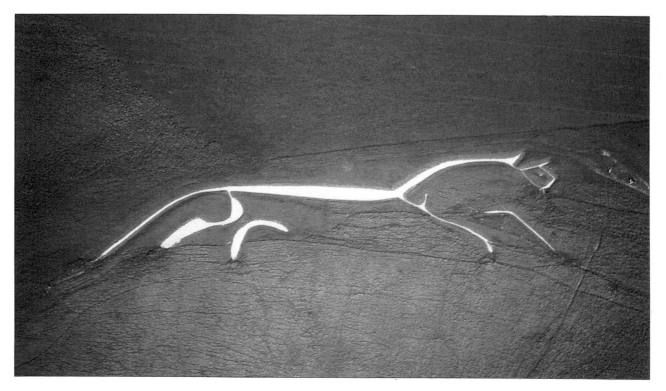

Modern miracles

Architects and artists in our own time create weird and wonderful works of art too.

Antonio Gaudí, a Spanish architect, designed many unusual buildings that you can see today in Barcelona. He hated straight lines, so his buildings, such as the apartment block Casa Milá, are based on natural things – shells, trees and flowers. The stonework is curved and rippled, the roof wiggles up and down like a wave and the chimneys look as if they have been squeezed from an icing nozzle. Casa Milá looks more like a building from a dream or a fairy story than a place where people really live.

In the United States, a cliff-face called Mount Rushmore has been carved with the faces of presidents of the USA. They are huge and glower impressively over the surrounding countryside, their mood seeming to change

▼ *This amazing building in Barcelona, Spain, is called the Templo de la Sagrada Familia, which means the cathedral of the Holy Family. It was designed by the Spanish architect Antonio Gaudí, who spent 40 years working on it but did not finish it. Even today it is not complete. Have you ever seen anything like it before? Gaudí used his imagination to create buildings that are unlike any others.*

▲ *These are the faces of four American presidents: George Washington, Thomas Jefferson, Franklin D. Roosevelt and Abraham Lincoln. It took a sculptor called Gutzon Borglum 13 years to make them. They are carved from the face of a mountain called Mount Rushmore in South Dakota, USA.*

with the weather and the time of day.

Christo is a contemporary artist with unusual ideas. He creates strange, temporary environments designed to catch your attention. He likes to wrap up public buildings and landscapes in sheets of plastic or fabric. In Australia he draped 24,000 square kilometres of coastline in plastic sheeting and named it *Wrapped Coast, Little Bay, Australia*. For *Running Fence*, he stretched 40 kilometres of white fabric across hills and into the sea. Because of the vast scale of some of these works, the full effect can only be seen from an aeroplane.

Seven Wonders of the Ancient World
Pyramids of Egypt
Statue of Zeus at Olympia
Colossus of Rhodes
Temple of Artemis at Ephesus
Mausoleum at Halicarnassus
Pharos at Alexandria
Hanging Gardens of Babylon

This list was made 2000 years ago by the Greek poet, Antiper of Sidon. He compiled it as a guide for travellers, rather like a modern guidebook. Sadly, all the Seven Wonders; except the pyramids, have now been destroyed. Look in your library for books with paintings of them.

Can you think of any buildings you would include in a list of modern wonders?

About the artists

BENTON, Thomas Hart (1889-1975) This American artist disliked modern, abstract painting and instead painted pictures with figures in them, often in rural settings.

BOSCH, Hieronymus (c. 1450-1516) Famous in his own lifetime, Netherlands artist Hieronymus Bosch painted solely religious pictures. His work is unique because it often refers to everyday life yet contains unusual, often grotesque, creatures.

BURRA, Edward (1905-1976) Although he painted many scenes of life in America, Spain and Mexico, Edward Burra was born in England. He painted many large watercolours, often of poor people and gangsters, and also designed stage sets for the theatre.

CAMPIN, ROBERT (c.1375-1444) This painter from the Netherlands was also called the Master of Flémalle. His paintings are very realistic and show many details of domestic life. He was the first artist to paint distant landscapes through open windows.

CHASE, William Merritt (1849-1916) Chase was an American artist who painted a variety of different subjects, from portraits to landscapes to still lifes.

CONSTABLE, John (1776-1837) This English painter was the first artist to paint landscape as it actually was. He achieved this by studying and sketching nature, using formal compositions and painting in an infinite variety of colours and shades.

DALI, Salvador (1904-1989) Not only did this Spanish artist paint symbolic, surreal landscapes, but he also designed jewellery and stage sets, wrote books and made films. He was famous for his technically brilliant and strangely disturbing pictures.

DERAIN, André (1880-1954) Derain was a French artist who considered colour to be the most important element of a painting. He painted using bright, often surprising, colours.

ERNST, Max (1891-1976) This German artist created fantastic pictures using not only paint but also pieces of wood, wallpaper and other bits and pieces. He also used frottage – a technique of placing a piece of paper over a rough surface such as bark and rubbing it with a crayon to create a textured finish.

GAUDI, Antonio (1852-1926) A Spanish architect who wanted to break away from the straight lines of modern architecture. Instead he turned to nature, and designed buildings using natural materials and based on natural curved shapes.

KUNISHAND (1786-1865) This Japanese artist produced thousands of beautiful prints, many of domestic scenes.

LORENZETTI, Ambrogio (c. 1300-1348) One of two Italian brothers, both of whom were painters. Ambrogio's best-known works are the frescoes called 'Good and Bad Government'.

LORRAIN, Claude (1600-1682) This French painter, whose real name was Claude Gelée, was most famous for his landscapes, many of which were painted in Italy. He closely studied light and made many sketches of the way it changes at dawn and dusk. Much of his work illustrates mythological and religious stories.

LOWRY, L.S. (1887-1976) An English painter, most famous for his pictures of bleak, industrial scenes in the North of England. These paintings are filled with 'matchstick' figures scurrying from place to place

MONET, Claude (1840-1926) Monet's paintings are composed of splashes of colour and have no dark outlines. He studied the effect of light on colour and often painted the same scene at different times of the day.

PISSARRO, Camille (1830-1903) A leading member of the French Impressionists, who tried to capture the 'impression' a scene made on the observer, rather than an accurate record.

ROGERS, Richard (1933-) An English architect known for his use of advanced technology and design in architecture. His most famous buildings are the Pompidou Centre, Paris, and the Lloyds Building, London.

ROUSSEAU, Henri, called 'Le Douanier' (1844-1910) A self-taught artist who worked as a customs official. He painted in a simple, imaginative style.

TURNER, Joseph Mallord William (1775-1851) An English painter, chiefly of landscapes. He began painting very young and was soon recognized as having great talent. In some of his paintings, the subject is obscured in a great swirl of light and colour.

VAN GOGH, Vincent (1853-1890) Although Van Gogh was a very influential artist, he sold only one painting during his lifetime. He suffered fits of madness and, during one of these, he cut off part of his ear. Two years later he shot himself. His paintings are full of brilliant colours and frenzied brushstrokes.

WOOD, Grant (1891-1942) An American painter, most famous for *American Gothic*. He painted in a very precise, stylized way.

WRIGHT, Frank Lloyd (1869-1959) An American architect whose most famous buildings include the Imperial Hotel, Tokyo, and the Guggenheim Museum in New York.

YOSHIMORY (1830-1884) A Japanese artist who specialized in designing wood-block prints of domestic scenes.

Acknowledgements

The National Trust Photographic Library / J. Whitaker, © National Trust 1991, p.6; The Metropolitan Museum of Art, Bequest of Miss Adelaide Milton de Groot (1876-1967), 1967 (67.187.123), p.17; ZEFA/DAMM, p.23; ZEFA/K. Goebel, p.26; ZEFA, pp.41 (top), 43, 44, 45; ZEFA/G. Sirena, p.41 (bottom); Michael Holford, p.24; Hutchison Library, p.25; Tate Gallery, London, p.31; Collection of Whitney Museum of American Art, New York, photography by Robert E. Mates Studio, N.J., p.39.

All other pictures are from the Bridgeman Art Library, courtesy of the following organizations: the Board of Trustees of the Victoria and Albert Museum, London, pp.7, 16, 38; Musée d'Orsay, Paris/Giraudon, p.8; Joslyn Museum, Omaha, p.9; Palazzo Pubblico, Siena, p.11; Pushkin Museum, Moscow, p.13; Tate Gallery, London, pp.14, 18; Tate Gallery/ © ADAGP, Paris and DACS, London, 1994, p.21; Lefevre Gallery, London/© Mrs Carol Ann Danes, p.15; The Fine Art Society, London, p.22; National Gallery, London, p.28 and *cover*; Prado, Madrid, pp.29, 35; Galerie Beycler, Basle, © SPADEM/ADAGP, Paris and DACS, London, 1994, p.30; Museum of Modern Art, New York, © DEMART PRO ARTE BV/DACS, 1994, p.32; Musée d'Orsay, Paris/Giraudon, p.37; Phillips, the International Fine Art Auctioneers, p.40.

The illustration on p.23 is by Annabel Spenceley; all other illustrations are by Tony Morris.

If copyright in any picture reproduced in this book has unwittingly been infringed, Touchstone Publishing Ltd apologizes and will pay an appropriate fee to the rightful owner as if we had been able to obtain prior permission.

Index